My First Book of Nature

Flowers

Victoria Munson

WINDMILL BOOKS

Published in 2019 by Windmill Books,
an Imprint of Rosen Publishing
29 East 21st Street, New York, NY 10010

Editor: Victoria Brooker
Book Design: Elaine Wilkinson

Photo Credits:
istock 19t Scacciamosche; Shutterstock: cover: (daffodil) Linda Yohler Photography; (poppy) Soyka; (daisy) barbol; (harebell) Svetlana Foote; (lily-of-the-valley) anyaivanova; (marsh marigold) tr3gin; (tulips) Kisialiou Yury; 2t rpt, 6b Paul Broadbent; 2-3 rpt, 10b Katarzyna Sobotka; 3t s_oleg; 3b rpt, 20b Gillian Holliday; 4 rpt, 4 BergeImLicht; 5t inlovepal; 5b cristalvi; 6t LUMIKK5550; 6-7 Artens; 7 Drozdowski; 8t Sann von Mai; 8B Sergei Drozd; 8-9 vladimir salman; 9 irin-k; 10t TuanZhariff; 10b wildswimmer; 11t Connor Howe; 11B Henrik Larsson; 12t neil hardwick; 12b Bob Pool, 13t&b, 18b Martin Fowler; Gert Hochmuth; 14b Kuttelvaserova Stuchelova; 15t Vasin Lee; 15b Mr Suwit Gaewsee-ngam; 16 Cyrustr; 17t fulgavlad; 17bHeike Rau; 18t Alina G; 19b HHelene; 20t Matt Gibson; 20b Gillian Holliday; 21t Chris Warham 21b Anton Sergeevich

Cataloging-in-Publication Data

Names: Munson, Victoria.
Title: Flowers / Victoria Munson.
Description: New York : Windmill Books, 2019. | Series: My first book of nature | Includes glossary and index.
Identifiers: LCCN ISBN 9781508196129 (pbk.) | ISBN 9781508196112 (library bound) | ISBN 9781508196136 (6 pack)
Subjects: LCSH: Flowers--Juvenile literature.
Classification: LCC QK49.M86 2019 | DDC 582.13--dc23

Manufactured in the United States of America

CPSIA Compliance Information: Batch #BS18WM:
For Further Information contact Rosen Publishing,
New York, New York at 1-800-237-9932

Contents

What Are Flowers?

Flowers are the part of a plant where seeds are made. Plants have several parts. The stem, or stalk, holds the flower up.

Petals are usually brightly colored to attract insects.

Flowers contain a sticky dust called pollen, which flowers need to help them make seeds.

Insects help to spread pollen as they move from flower to flower looking for food.

Flowers can be found in all kinds of habitats, such as in woods, on mountains, and even in water.

Never pick wildflowers. Leave them so that other people can enjoy them, too.

Garden Flowers

In early spring, colorful daffodils bloom. These bright yellow, funnel-shaped flowers sit on the end of tall, hollow stems.

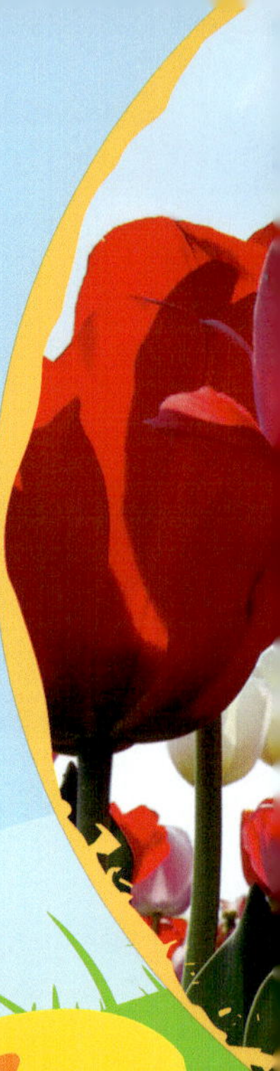

There are at least 25 species of daffodils.

The butterfly bush has a very sweet smell. The flower heads are long and look like purple bushy tails.

Butterflies are often found on butterfly bushes.

Tulips can be almost any color. The large, thick petals point upwards, opening out in bright sunshine.

The Netherlands exports 2 million tulips every year!

Several centuries ago in Holland, tulips were more valuable than gold.

Lavender has small purple flowers clustered at the top of long, thin stems.

At the end of summer, some people collect lavender flowers to make scented bags for drawers and cupboards.

Wildflowers

Clover has clusters of tiny white or pink flowers on thin, upright stems. It has three round leaves that are marked with a pale "V" shape.

Dandelions have bright yellow flower heads.

In late summer, dandelion flower heads turn into seeds. Blow them away and make a wish!

Buttercups are poisonous for cows and sheep, so they know to avoid them.

Buttercups have shiny, bright yellow petals.

Daisies have small white petals around a yellow center. The name daisy comes from the phrase "day's eye," because they close at night and open in the daytime.

Daisies are found everywhere on Earth except Antarctica.

Seashore Flowers

Beach morning glory flowers open in the morning and close before noon.

The beach morning glory is actually a vine. It can grow up to 75 feet (23 m) long! Sometimes it is called "goat's foot creeper."

Sea thrift grows on beaches.

Sea thrift is also called "sea pink" because of its pretty flowers.

Beach sunflowers grow in sand dunes.

Beach sunflowers look similar to regular sunflowers, but they are much smaller.

Beach peas have long, drooping purple flowers and oval leaves.

In the summer, pea-like seeds grow in pods.

Beach peas are also called sea peas.

Mountain Flowers

Common milkwort flowers can be dark blue, pink, or white.

Milkwort's small flowers cluster at the end of the stem. It has narrow, pointed leaves.

Fairy slipper orchids are a bright rosy purple.

Each stem grows a single slipper-shaped flower.

Wild thyme has purple-pink flowers.

Wild thyme grows well in many different habitats, not just on mountains.

Thyme has a strong lemony smell.

Heath speedwell is a tall plant with pale purple petals.

The Romans used speedwell as medicine.

Water Flowers

The yellow flag iris grows beside rivers and lakes. Its leaves are tall and sword shaped.

The yellow flag iris got its name because its drooping petals look like flags.

Yellow marsh marigolds grow in clumps of flowers near water.

Water lily flowers are usually white or light pink, but can also be orange, blue, or red.

Water lilies sit among lily pads floating on ponds or lakes.

Water lily flowers look like star-shaped cups.

Water lily leaves can grow up to 6 feet (2 m) wide.

Meadow Flowers

Lupines grow all over North America.

Bees are attracted to colorful flowers.

Lupines can fill entire fields with their pretty colors. They come in shades of blue, pink, and purple.

Field bindweed is a pretty, sweet-smelling flower. However, it is also a pest for farmers because it has long roots that are very hard to get rid of.

Look closely at a bindweed's stem. It wraps itself tightly around other plants for support.

Common mallow has pink petals with dark purple lines on them.

The ancient Romans used to grow mallow for food and medicine.

Bog Flowers

Heather is a small plant that grows close to the ground. Its tough, woody stems grow upright and are covered in lots of tiny pinky-purple flowers.

Heather twigs can be used to make brooms, baskets, rope, and bedding.

Bog asphodel gets its name because it is found growing in bogs. When the flowers turn to fruit, the stems turn dark orange.

Bog asphodel has yellow, star-like flowers.

Butterwort is a purple-petaled, insect-catching plant. The bright yellow-green leaves have a sticky liquid on them that insects like.

When an insect comes to eat the liquid, it gets trapped. The plant closes its leaves around the insect and digests it.

Butterwort is also known as bog violet.

Grass-of-Parnassus is also known as "bog star" because it is found mainly in wet and boggy habitats.

Grass-of-Parnassus has white flowers with green stripes.

Forest Flowers

In the spring, forest floors are covered with hundreds of bluebells.

Bluebell flowers are small, drooping, bluish-purple bell shapes.

Flowering in spring means bluebells can get the most sunlight before the trees are covered in leaves.

Foxgloves are tall plants covered in 20–30 bell-shaped, pinky-purple flowers.

Ramsons is also known as wild garlic because if you crush the leaves they smell like garlic.

Ramsons flowers have six pointed white petals.

Lily-of-the-valley is a sweet-scented plant with tiny, bell-shaped white flowers.

Lily-of-the-valley has large, bright green leaves.

Its fruit is a small orange berry that holds brown seeds.

Dandelion Life Cycle

Dandelion seeds are attached to tiny, parachute-type stalks that are light enough to float in the wind.

1. A seed flies through the air.
2. The seed lands on soil.
3. A root starts to grow down.
4. A shoot grows up to the light.

5

The leaves and roots grow bigger and stronger.

6

The buds turn into flower heads.

7

The flowers turn to seeds, which are blown away in the wind. The life cycle begins again.

Glossary and Index

bog an area of soft, wet, muddy ground

export to sell to other countries

flower head a blossom or cluster of small flowers at the top of a stem

habitat a place where a plant or an animal lives in the wild

pollen the powder found in flowers